More tips for new teachers

A further set of ideas for survival

Ian Windsor

More tips for new teachers
A further set of ideas for survival

First Print Edition

Published by Ian Windsor
ISBN 978-0-9575181-2-4

All Content © Ian Windsor 2017.

About Me

I teach science and have worked in a number of secondary schools in the UK. I've been Head of Science in my current school for a few years and alongside my main subject I have also taught citizenship, music and technology.

I'm an experienced mentor and professional tutor for colleagues in the early stages of their teaching career. I have worked with colleagues on PGCE, and a number of school-based ITE routes and with NQTs in a variety of subjects.

I also work as a visiting lecturer delivering physics subject knowledge enhancement courses for colleagues both in ITE and further stages of their careers.

Introduction

Since the publication of the first book of 100 tips, the number of ways that one can enter the profession has diversified. There are increased options for employment-based routes into teaching and also a focus on higher level reflective practice throiugh the academic teacher training routes.

Whichever route you follow, the core messages remain, and the relationships you establish are still central to everything.

Good luck – Make it the rewarding career it can be.

Ian Windsor. November 2017

Are they ready to learn if they've been out in the rain?

Rain – the ruin of breaktime for those staff called to wet break duty. How on earth will you get that last minute photocopying done now?

But spare a thought for your poor pupils if they're soaking wet. Getting dry and warm is going to be foremost on their mind, not the learning outcomes you've planned so meticulously.

Maslow's hierarchy of needs rings true. Pupils need so be ready to learn. Things like being sheltered, fed, and not needing the loo are fundamental to the quality of learning that your pupils experience.

More Maslow.

He's good you know.

Assuming that your pupils are fed and watered and cool enough / warm enough (delete as applicable depending on whether today's date is the UK's annual hot day, or the rest of the year), the next stage is to ensure that they are working safely in a safe environment.

On from that, if you can foster a collaborative ethos of mutual respect and support – you'll be hitting most of Maslow's criteria for optimum learning to take place.

Maybe after lunch you could have a go at addressing cold fusion followed by third world debt before bed time!

Seriously though – It's all these things which lead to pupils high self-esteem – so lacking in many of them. High self-esteem leads to confidence which leads to all that creative, problem solving and success.

Busy from the beginning.

A purposeful start to the lesson sets the tone for the rest of it. Have something for the students to do from the moment they enter the classroom. Even better if it links to the learning from the previous lesson with you. Activities focused around key-word ideas are good too. Any opportunity to build literacy in shouldn't be wasted.

Make these activities short, fairly easy to achieve and to last no more than five minutes. It's very easy for this initial activity to take up much more lesson time than you anticipate.

Buddies.

There will be pupils who play up.

The way you 'set your stall out' initially can overcome some of this and consistent application of your rules will soon send a message out as to what students can expect to be like in your lesson.

Good planning can overcome part of it too.

But there'll still be naughty kids…

Having a buddy – maybe someone in the next classroom to yours, who'll have someone off your hands is essential. Getting persistent bad behavior out of the room before it ruins the lesson is very important.

Follow it up with the correct sanctions and school procedures

Class detention.

Setting a whole-class detention needs really careful consideration. Is it that every member of the class has warranted being in detention? How does it make them feel? Does it pick out the individual causes of the problems? Does it show the students that you don't really know who's who?

Be firm, but fair.

There's always a reason.

There are always things going on people's lives. Sometimes these things are far more important than your lesson. The difference between us and the kids is that as adults and professionals, we have to isolate other issues in our lives and get on with the job. Most kids find that virtually impossible.

You may be told some background information about students if you need to know it. In many cases there will be staff in school who know much more sensitive and often harrowing confidential information. In other cases, the school won't know anything.

In every case you must report things. The school will have people and procedures to deal with it. Someone will be collating this information and working to support that child.

Be mindful of this when so-and-so is not doing what you want. What else might be going on for them?

What and when to mark.

The school will have a marking policy outlining the expectations. In many cases, the policy will follow a model of 'light touch' marking of class work and notes and a more thorough focus on specific pieces of work. This targeted marking should be aimed at work which will the student to use a wide-range of concepts and ideas. Ideally an open-ended question would be the starting point.

Write comments on the work and get the students to respond to the comments and improve on their work.

Students' work.

Students' work – be it written in books, in electronic form or in the form of some creative process is the prime evidence of how successful your classroom is.

The key word here is 'progress'. Do you know what progress your students make? If other people want to see what progress is like in your classroom they'll look over the last few months' work in those books.

If you're following the marking ideas from the previous page, the students will be making progress.

Verbal feedback.

Conversations between teachers and students happen all the time. In many cases these will involve moving the student's work along to a greater depth or higher level of work.

Is this worth noting in their work? The green pens come useful again here where students can make a quick note of how they can improve following their discussion with you. Some schools use 'verbal feedback' rubber stamps where the students write their note next to the stamp. If there's no stamp I guess you could just write the initials 'VF' as long as it doesn't translate badly into anything you should be avoiding!

How big is your writing?

A simple – but obvious tip. If you're using a white board to write on, how neat is your writing? How big is it? Is the pen ink vivid enough to be read?

It's worth a practice to get this right.

Also check that the board isn't too shiny for certain places in the room due to reflections of the light from windows etc.

How's your voice?

How well do you project your voice? Have you found the key to talking to the whole room and the key to talking when the the class are gathered around you? Ask the students at the back if they can hear ok.

Know the time.

Quite often you'll find a real determination to get through everything you want to and a couple of scenarios may develop:

In some cases you'll rush ahead with the content of the lesson and go at such a pace that students just don't learn things along the way. It's much more important to ensure that they're 'getting it'.

This leads to another situation where you may find yourself at the end of the lesson before you've done everything you needed.

Covering everything isn't the most important thing. You can pick it up next lesson as long as time running away doesn't become a recurring theme. Build your lessons from the main points that you want the students to learn and as you gain experience you'll ensure that what you put into that lesson won't cause it to overrun.

Go on a trip.

If there's a trip running somewhere and you're asked to go and if you can make it, go.

There's an increasing amount of legislation around school trips – as is quite right, and there'll be someone in your school who is the visits coordinator. They won't let the trip take place until all of the risk assessments and paperwork is done. Once you're out on the trip learn how the main organizer has set things up and you never know, you might be leading one soon.

Meet and greet.

Simple this one – Be at your classroom door to welcome the students into the lesson. You can check their uniform etc. You can give out any starter activity and also guide them towards the frame of mind you want them in for your lesson.

A quick thought while I was writing this page:

Is it their lesson? Your lesson? Our lesson?

Is it their classroom? Your classroom etc.

I don't suppose there's a right or wrong answer here. These all have a small effect on the quality of learning that takes place.

Talk is cheap.

Let the students talk.

The best thing is if they're talking about the work they're doing. If they can talk about it, they can go a long way to getting it down on paper. If you've used keyword lists, make sure that the students use those words in their conversations.

The arrangement of the tables in your room goes a long way to encouraging conversations and groupwork.

Individual work too.

So just to go against everything on the previous page, time for quiet individual work is precious too. Make the expectations clear for all of these different 'learning times'. The students will soon get used to it.

Variety is the key, well, organized variety.

A picture paints a thousand words.

It's amazing how much a picture from an internet search can do for you. You might ask students to comment on it, use it for the basis of some creative writing, art, music, pros and cons for history, geography, science.

Using a three by three grid of nine photos is a nice way of doing an open ended questions. Ask the students to link three things with similarities or differences, or pick the odd one out. There's no definitive right or wrong of course but the students will find lots of correct answers and the discussions can go from there.

Roll the dice...

Bringing a random element to the setting of activities in lessons can be a strong motivational tool.

Try laying out a six by six grid and using two dice. The grid could contain thirty-six different activities.

It could contain just six activities in rows (one dice) which get harder as you progress left to right across the columns (the second dice).

This sets up some nice differentiation. You need to ensure though that the work that's 'rolled' is of a suitable level of challenge so involve the child once the dice have been rolled. Ask them if they think that the challenge they've been set is ok for them. Do they need to change it?

Thinking about the level of challenge and always trying to push on a little bit is an important mindset to try and get students to adopt.

We're all human.

Of course we are.

Learn from every experience.

Build on what's already there.

It won't be fully right the first time.

It probably won't be the second time either.

But it'll get there if you want it to.

Now is this written for the students or you?

Time of day.

When you're presented with your timetable, it's a good idea to look at where you have each particular class. You could then make the decision as to when to set homework, collect in books for marking etc. and establish that routine quite quickly.

It might also be worth considering what type of activities you plan to run in lessons. Some groups will respond and perform better at certain times of the school day and certain activities lend themselves more readily to different parts of the day too.

Instant success.

Success is becoming increasingly instant for a lot of schoolchildren and there are arguments that a young person's resilience is reducing. The challenges you present to the students will not yield instant gratification in many cases and it's very easy for the students to give up before they've tried.

What balance between quick achievable goals and the more long-term deep set learning are you setting?

Tailoring marking.

Students like to know what they're aiming for. When setting a piece of work, it's sometimes a good idea to share the marking criteria with them. What do they have to do to get the marks? How will they have to present their ideas to not lose out?

This can be extended into marking of each-others' work and be used to develop a more thorough understanding of how to use and present their knowledge and understanding.

Awe and Wonder.

Awe and wonder used to be banded around as a phrase in inspections. If you got a collective 'wow' from your students during a lesson observation you've won.

Guess what – forget the lesson observation, just try and get a collective wow anyhow. As much as you can.

Then what you do with that moment immediately after is the important bit. You've got the attention and the wondering minds, now build on it.

Speak.

Sometimes people don't speak in the corridor. Even something as basically civil as 'good morning', or thanking you when you hold the door for them. If they're like this with colleagues they'll undoubtedly be like this with children.

They're usually the ones who complain most about rude pupils too.

Chunking.

When you're faced with a teaching a new topic to a class:

What are you expecting the students to already be able to do?

What's the order in which the concepts need to be learned?

What needs to be known first?

What examples can reinforce students' ideas?

How will assess each step of the topic?

Can you assess the whole topic towards the end other than using a test?

All of this is underpinned by breaking things down into small manageable chunks. Sometimes the breaking down of our ideas from degree level requires a lot of thought.

Phones.

Phones are a massively contentious issue in schools. There are many negative aspects of phone use in school from disruption through to child protection issues and school will have a policy regarding their use.

If your school does allow the use of mobiles, there are a number of really positive benefits. Some examples are listed below:

Photo's of example work from the board or a working area to refer to individually.

Video footage of techniques in PE, music performances or experiments in science. In many cases video evidence can be submitted as coursework.

App use and evaluation for ICT.

All of these can be done in aeroplane mode (I can't bring myself to write 'airplane mode' sorry!), however research will require connection and can lead to other issues. Like everything it'll be how you manage it – as long as the use of phones is permitted.

Bad Language.

Swearing is unacceptable.

The kids will swear, you'll probably feel like it too! But it's the escalation of the issue that can cause real problems.

Was it in response to something like a loud bang?

Was it part of their conversation? For some people the f-word is by far their most widely used adjective and adverb.

Was it directed at someone else?

Was it aggressive towards someone else?

Was it about you?

And many more…

As I said, swearing is unacceptable but the context defines how you deal with it. A sharp reminder from you or a referral through the school system?

How to research.

One area where I've found that teachers' expectations differ greatly from students' abilities is in researching. I think that an aspect of it is due to the fact that teachers have likely studied at university level and have had to produce papers and dissertations that are fully researched and correctly referenced.

Without guidance, many of your students will 'research' something by cutting and pasting large swathes of website content. The level of language is the usual giveaway. Of course this can't be done but you could direct them to a handful of websites and ask them to pick out five positive and five negative points (as an example). Your students will need some really strict research instructions initially until they've learned how to do it properly.

Assessment against exam targets.

The school experience should be so much more than learning to pass exams. At some stage however, the students will need to align their way of expressing their ideas with the requirements of the exam board.

In the UK, the changes to GCSE and A-levels through 2016-2018 have given us slightly different exam criteria however the exam papers from previous years are still an invaluable resource for practicing for the exams. Most subjects and exam boards publish past papers, mark schemes and examiner reports on their websites and there are example assessments available for the new specifications as well as the library of past papers which will increase as time goes on.

From my experience, there's a strong correlation between success and students who engage with these papers from an early stage of their revision.

Of course, sticking at these papers can be disheartening, sometimes it takes 4 or 5 attempts at different papers before a student sees their percentages begin to increase. They'll need a lot of nurturing from you. In many cases it might be worth considering putting a plan together for them.

Putting things right.

Learning which is personalised to an individual student addresses their needs with great effect. It's difficult to instigate and one of the reasons for this is that you as the teacher will be effectively letting go of some of your control of the classroom.

Students may be all working on different parts of the work of even different topics and there will have to be a great deal of your trust in them to do this. You'll also need to get around them quickly during the lesson and be able to field questions on whatever may arise during the session.

Identifying areas for students to work on is also tricky. During revision some students will shy away from working at topics they find difficult and tend to play it safe. There's a balance to be struck here between their confidence and them widening their ideas.

Sometimes a test paper is good starting point where areas the student has performed less well are identified and some work set to develop these areas.

Quiz Time.

A quick quiz during the lesson is a good way of checking the learning that's taking place and also breaks up the activities in the lesson. Students can work individually or in teams – you choose.

From experience it's probably better to use closed questions (which only have one or a few possible answers), as the marking can get time consuming.

This is also a nice activity to do if you find yourself needing to fill a few minutes during a lesson.

The start of the next lesson.

Don't make the assumption that your students will have remembered every detail from their previous lesson with you. They will remember many things and with prompting will remember other things too but you must be mindful that they've had lots of other lessons and their lives going on between now and their previous lesson with you.

It's a good idea to start the lesson with with something which draws on the students' prior learning in your subject. Just a few minutes to blow the cobwebs off those facts and ideas that they covered last time.

Learn names.

This is so important. I've heard stories of teachers not knowing the name of the child sitting with in front of them with mom and dad at parents' evening. That's bad, but so is not knowing their name in the lesson. Many schools will have photographs on the school network or management system software. Use a seating plan if you want to.

Some people use a set of names on cards or lollipop sticks in lessons to choose pupils to answer questions. It all helps you to learn those names.

Getting this done quickly helps add to building the relationship between you and your students

Find your position.

Classroom routines needs to be quickly established in the first few weeks of taking a class. One point to consider is where you stand or sit in your room.

If you want to get the whole group's attention it's useful to have a standard phrase such as "stop and listen please", spoken in a standard manner and delivered from a certain physical point in the room. All of this will help your routine of getting attention and addressing the class.

How you stand is important too. You may need a level of authoritative assertion here and your posture and demeanor will go a long way to support this.

Changing tasks.

In many situations the most confusion and disruption to the smooth running of a lesson can take place at the point where the group is moving from one task to another.

If the members of the class are physically moving during these stages the problem can be compounded.

These changes need to be made clear. If you're using powerpoint, a slide could be displayed which clearly states the current activity. If students are all working independently at their own pace, a list could be used with new activities available.

Think about having monitors to hand out and collect in equipment too.

Equipped to learn.

You will get a number of students in your classes who won't have the basic equipment. It's usually a school expectation for students to arrive at school equipped and because of this it's also very easy to become embroiled in an argument over a student not having a pen.

Of course this will need logging and their form-tutor notified (if this is the school procedure), but for the smooth progress of your lesson, it's a very useful idea to have a pack of pens, pencils etc. ready to hand out.

The same goes for paper if the students don't bring books. Follow the procedures for not having equipment (which may be a detention etc.), but sort the 'here and now' out and let them get on with the learning you want them to do today.

The bell is a sign for me, not for you.

Very true, but you need to make sure that the lesson ending is clear.

Some students will start to move when the bell goes, get them sat down and not fiddling with bags or books.

Go over the main learning points, ask questions, look for shows of hands.

Try and time it so that this plenary section is taking place as the bell goes. A crisp, productive end is just as important as the rest of the lesson and it's difficult to achieve sometimes when you're at the tail end of the previous hour's work.

Encourage all the way.

It's very easy (and probably just human nature), to criticize all the negatives that students will bring along to lessons: lack of effort, bad behaviour, not being bothered etc.

And you have to deal with it following the school procedures but you also need to realise that you're going to have that student every lesson in most cases and while establishing the boundaries for what you'll accept or not will work some way, you also need to – in the words of one colleague, "be the adult here".

Just like the continued consistent reinforcement of your expectations will improve things, recognition of all the positive things going on (and there will be), is probably more important. Just encourage everything. If it's the work they've done – great. If they've stayed in their seats longer today than last lesson – fab. If they've sat and worked for the last 15 minutes after a telling off – superb.

Make sure you put your praise in context – be specific. Let the students know what you think that they've done is good and over time there will be a shift.

Go on and on and on.

Keep reinforcing the key points you want your students to learn. These will be the overarching ideas of the lesson. You'll probably have set your students a variety of different activities which reinforce or apply these ideas.

This is the key: What do they know at the end of the lesson that they didn't at the start.

Have I mentioned this before?

Turn the tables

Have a think about the layout of your classroom. Do you want all of the tables arranged so that the pupils are all facing you and the board? Do you want the tables set out for pupils to face ach other and do groupwork? Can the tables be re-arranged during the lesson depending on what activity you want to do? Promoting the right kind of conversation between your pupils is important.

The right kind of guidance.

Sometimes work is set along the lines of 'read page 34 and answer the questions'. This might have followed a discussion or presentation to the class.

Have a think about providing a variety of resources – electronically or paper-based, which students could use and look up ideas to help them explain their understanding of the work they're doing. This follows on from the open questioning mentioned earlier. I suppose it could be called 'open resourcing'.

Share what success looks like.

Students will produce better work if they know what they're aiming for. It's a good idea to let them look at good and poor examples of work and understand why that work has been awarded the marks it has.

This can be set up for virtually any piece of work and is a skill invaluable to the students by the time they come to revise using past papers, mark schemes and examiners' reports.

Take note.

One task which becomes almost second nature to students in higher education is the ability to make good notes.

Students in school will need a lot of guidance as to what is important to note and how to note it. A pro-forma of some sort would be invaluable. This would help students to focus on specific areas and guide them to note the important things you want them to note.

Structured templates for focusing students' thoughts and ideas make a huge difference to the learning which takes place in your lessons.

Vocabulary.

Think about how you can get your students to incorporate the required language into their work for you. One method is to set up a keywords dictionary – perhaps in the form of a small notebook, with correct spellings and definitions of keywords.

Each lesson can have a keywords element and those new words can be added to the dictionary at some point.

As a further extension of the idea, students could highlight or underline the keywords when they use them in their work.

Use the keywords in discussions at all times.

Get rich quick.

Using wide open or 'rich' questions with a group is a great way of starting a discussion. Even if it's just a statement - for example 'the sun isn't going to shine for a year', that can trigger all sorts of discussion – on or off topic.

Letting creativity happen is of paramount importance. You'll have to referee though and make sure that discussions don't get silly but most of the time the group dynamic keeps discussions rooted in reality.

These discussions can lead to some great group or individual work and can provide excellent opportunities for students to draw on their wide-range of knowledge and understanding. The more links they can make between topics, the more they'll understand.

Keep Checking.

Keep checking your students understanding every ten minutes or so. This could be by stopping the class as a whole and getting something like a show of hands or looking around at the students individually.

It doesn't have to be restricted to the lesson time either. Stop them in the corridors or other times that you see them. Not in a threatening way of course, just a light-hearted 'tell me this' kind of way.

Confidence.

You need it and you must also do your best to instill it in the students you teach. Encouragement is so important for everyone – whatever the stage of their life or studies.

Even if you don't feel like your confidence is flowing, you'll still need to maintain that air in front of your students.

Your subject's not for everyone.

Not every child is going to find Hooke's law, Macbeth, the civil war, trigonometry etc. as thrilling as you may. The key is to appeal to as many as you can through making it straightforward to navigate through, by setting up a problem and solving it and letting the pupils have some sense of success using and applying whatever they've learned today. Don't make it be a bring wall. They'll just bang their heads up it.

Teach something you don't know.

If you get chance, try something out of your comfort zone of knowledge. Sometimes you can see easier routes into topics and concepts that you're learning at the same time. This is the opposite of the idea of breaking down something you know inside-out into a logical order. Sometimes planning to teach something you're learning too is easier.

Names on sticks

One way of learning pupils' names as well as randomizing questioning is to have them all written on lollipop sticks and drawn out of a pot. You'll quickly learn all of the names and everyone will stay on their toes in case they're picked to answer the question.

It doesn't have to be sticks although I guess that they're relatively cheap. Anyway of including everyone is a good thing.

Keep going

We're forever telling our students to keep plugging away at something, to keep asking, to think about things, to pull ideas apart, to practice applying ideas and evaluate how well they've done. We offer endless advice about balancing work and recreation and how small moves performed often will lead to improved success.

That applies to us too. It's not all plain sailing, teaching's got its fair share of red tape and ridiculous demands which pull us away from what we're meant to be doing and the system survives on goodwill and generosity.

Not a job that's easy if you're not into it. It's amazing how many people bemoan the amount of time which the kids are off school but in the next breath tell you how they couldn't / wouldn't do your job in a million years.

Enjoy yourselves!

If you've found this book useful, please check out its predecessor 'New to teaching – 100 Tips for Survival', and find us on facebook.

Thanks for reading.

Ian.

www.ingramcontent.com/pod-product-compliance
Lightning Source LLC
Chambersburg PA
CBHW051047030426
42339CB00006B/236